C000098364

BETTER LATE THAN NEVER TO GO TO HELL

JOHN GUNKY

Copyright © 2023 by John Gunky

Paperback: 978-1-959224-44-0
eBook: 978-1-959224-45-7
Library of Congress Control Number: 2023900934

All rights reserved. No part of this publication may be reproduced, distributed, or
transmitted in any form or by any electronic or mechanical means, without the prior
written permission of the publisher, except in the case of brief quotations embodied
in critical reviews and certain other noncommercial uses permitted by copyright law.

Ordering Information:

Prime Seven Media
518 Landmann St.
Tomah City, WI 54660

Printed in the United States of America

TABLE OF CONTENTS

⌗ Mother's tears ⌗

There was nothing to do at his hood
So he left home real soon
Worked here and there untill he got bored…
Shaved his head and he got wrong.
When he signed in and enrolled
He was blind and young
Getting army brainwashed
Mother's tears
For her son on war
Just learning how to get commanded
Fighting for another man
Playing chess war with your heart
Is like a blind man throwing darts
Maybe you won't never come back
To see your winning mom
That she is praying her Lords
For you not to return in a pine box
Mother's tears
For her son on war
Shooting bullets with a dirty gun
Never aim with the right hand
On a target where poor is the dead
When the money rules never care
For the anger the fear and the rage
Of the one who kills to be save
Hate feeds hate that's the same
Everywhere you fight you blame!!!
Mother's tears
For her son on war

⧣ Blind Love ⧣

Sex symbol in the neighborhood

Walking stumbling on her new shoes

Stabbing other's people back!!!

Making my Bird to shut up ¡!!

Drinking alone in the pub

Waiting for you to return

With your hips, moves, with style and look

Work and believe in your thoughts

That will make you strong

Why don't you let free my young soul

Letting speak my mind

The way I feel and I want....

Getting in your house with my dog

Sorry for knocking on your door

1,2,3… I just wanna see you fuck ¡!!

I just wanna see you guys fucking out there

No worries I don't like

Your ugly models make of plastic for love

Envy and vanity kill the world

Sorry for hitting you so strong

I didn't mean it, to finish with your love

I only want you to pick up the phone

When I call…

Blind love…

Flemish love…

The wildest one…

Attitude is all I've got

Nothing is more valuable than my soul.

Convictions lost all day alone

Going back over my neighborhood

Welkome over my BRIXTON rules

Going over my nigga's hood

1,2,3…. I just wanna see you fuck!!!

I just wanna see you guys fucking out there….

PEACE, LOVE, UNITY, RESPECT

PEACE, LOVE, UNITY, RESPECT

♯ Singing Under The Rain ♯

It's gonna rain again
Thunders lights and hail
I'm ready for the chase
Running far away
To your love slay.
Singing Under The Rain
Before my leaving train
Singing Under The Rain
Breaking up the chain
It's gonna rain again
No matter what you say
I won't go insane.
I'm only feeling pain
My love is not the same
Singing Under The Rain
Before my leaving train
Breaking up the chain
It's gonna rain again!!!
Please don't talk in vain
Things I have to blame
Words are blown away
Nothing else to say
It's gonna rain again

♯ Bolonia's Wind ♯

Bolonia's Wind
Makes me think
It's like a dream
Stand by me
Thousands life
Will can not explain
What harvest moon
Can makes me feel
Sweet memories....
Bolonia's Wind
Smells like weed
Stand by me
Puff, Puff Give!!!
Mountain truth
Are shaman's rules
The wild weed
Smoke it free
Sweet memories
Bolonia's Wind
Smells like weed
Stand by me
Puff, Puff Give!!!
Magick tin with LSD
I can see ...
What you can feel.
Bolonia's Wind
Smells like weed.

Puff, Puff Give!!!
Pass a hit to me
Come with me
I'll make you feel
As a queen, in Bolonia's beach
Ashes rest in peace!!!

⌗ Sleeping Under ⌗

Cuban cane

Sugar love

Summer songs

Sleeping Under

Thousands stars

If you go

Please come back

Sleeping Under

Big blue moon

Magick shrooms

I want some too

Sleeping Under, yeah

Guitar jam

Fire bums

Shooting stars

Sleeping Under

Fresh cold dawn

Nice and calm

I'm feeling damped

Sleeping Under

Cuban cane

Sugar love

Morning songs

Sleeping Under

✚ Pray No More ✚

From love to hate
There's only one step
Please shed no tears
That I don't deserve
Don't start a fight
Without a good end
Keep your rage
Inside of yourself
Leave me alone
Please pray no more
Leave me alone
Please cry no more
Just take your shit
Is hard to deal with
You've been so mean
So that's what you get
Why don't get lost
and leave me alone
'Cause all I want
Is to stand on my own
Leave me alone
Please pray no more
Leave me alone
Please cry no more
Please don't lie
Face life as you like
My love is gone

And this war is lost
Do no shit
You later regret
I don't break down
In this crazy world
Leave me alone
Please pray no more
Leave me alone
Please cry no more

⚡ Opium Solstice ⚡

Poppy's seeds
Opium dreams
Twilight zone
On pagan's moon
Waiting for
Poppy's silk
Like mother's milk
Golden route
Years of war
Against natural rules
Poppy's seeds
Opium dreams
Hippocratic society
Opium Solstice
Summer joy
Indian rush
You are my healer
Take me deep
Inside your
Opium dreams
When you go
Down to sleep
Faithful like a dog
I wanna be....
Poppy's seeds
Opium dreams
Hippocratic society

Oh Sweet Matron

Oh sweet matron
Coming to see me
Lunch time break
Big smile in her face
Oh sweet matron
Coming to pet me
Great blue eyes
I can read inside
Oh sweet matron
Coming to see me
When I cry
Come next to me
Oh sweet matron
Coming to pet me
Love feelings
From picis heart
Oh sweet matron
Coming to see me
Oh sweet matron
Coming to pet me
Oh sweet matron
Coming to love me

⚓ Never Came Back ⚓

Learnt from look at the moon
Waiting for you coming soon
'Crossed the window of my room
As a witch on her broom
Following the shooting stars
Welkome to never ever land
Where you won't never come back
Unless you find your own ticket to return
You never came back
From never land
Wait untill you grow up
Babe you'll be another one
That wants to be a man
Before learning to run
Why have you gone so far
After you broke up the glass
Welkome to never ever land
Where you won't never return
You never came back
From never land
Babe if you ever return
With a rose in your hand
Just before we break up
It's better to have a little fun
Dancing around in the sun
Rolling all over the grass
Welkome to never ever land
Where you won't never return
From never land

⚓ Second hand smoke ⚓

Waking up
Feeling burnt
You fire me up
Second hand love
Second hand smoke
I'm feeling trash
You are like a slash
In my hands
Second hand love
Second hand smoke
Day and night
Babe you are so tight
I feel alright
Second hand love
Second hand smoke
You are my queen
I'm your pimp
As you can see
Second hand love
Second hand smoke
Can't break my heart
It's like ice rock
You fucking snob
Second hand love
Second hand smoke
Going home
Traffic jam
I'm fucking alone
Second hand love
Second hand smoke

Istanbul's moonshine

Like a man on his knees
When he just
Breakdown in war
Other man's war ¡!!
When there's nothing to lose
It's time to throw away
Your dirty old shoes…
Dirty old shoes!!!
Since we don't sit and smoke
My life went
Out of control…
Out of control!!!
And I never felt
Real…..
Love anymore
Love anymore!!!!
It's alright
Istanbul's full moon
Rock dirty rules
Jamming the blues
Old Navy rules
No problem at all
Everything can be sold but my soul
Can't get my soul ¡!!
Even if evil says
I can get
All I want
Get all I want ¡!!
'Cause nothing was

Said on time
To mad Mr DOUGH
MAD MR DOUGH!!!
I smoke libanés
Since I'm fucking
18 years old
18 years old ¡!!
It's alright
Istanbul's full moon
Rock dirty rules
Old Navy rules
Jamming the blues
Lies change opinions
From people zapping
On TV control
Remote control!!!
This guy's are jamming
Good rock and roll
At the end of the day
We can change it
If we really want
We really want!!!
Jamming alone
Jimi Hendrix
Love songs
It's alright
Istanbul's full moon
Rock dirty rules
Jamming the blues

♯ Beach Bum Blues ♯

I'm a beach bum
Day and night
I'm drinking in the bar
No matter where I go
I end up having fun
Because I always find
Something to burn
Smoking the roach
I'm having head rush
I'm a beach bum
You are like a joker
Please don't make me laugh
Why you gave me
A coin for good luck
I'm going to the sea
Before I get drunk
To wait for a wave
To get a good surf
I'm a beach bum
I'm a bit stoned
After hitting the bong
I'm so high dude
Leave me alone
I can't jam
I forgot all my songs
Because I'm whistling
The beach bum blues
I'm a beach bum

⚓ Budweiser Dream ⚓

I think
You are to me
As donkey piss
Since I drunk
The real malt
The fuzzy beer
Makes me think
I'm like
A drunk ass pimp
Looking in my pockets
For my Lost soul
That I don't know
If I sold it
To wicked devil
Or I pawned it
For another love
Your love blinds me
Like a cold blonde
I can't reckon if..
This is blues or rock and roll
On the corner pub
Musical crossroads
After 100 pints spilled
On the floor
The waiter is looking anger
Because we don't
Even say hello

Showing no respect
Wicked devil 😼
We love jamming Rock an roll!!!
Once I have a dream
We were pouring pints
Of the real malt
Litting the oil lamp
That leads us the way
To the next pub
Your love blinds me
Like a cold blonde
I can't reckon if
This is blues or rock and roll ¡!!

⌗ Love Stinks ⌗

Money and women don't get on well
I don't mind the way you smell
Never care what clothes you wear
Perfums, diamonds make you fresh
Babe don't you know beauty is in the heart…
So lay down and just relax
Money and women don't get on well
They are never happy 100 percent
Love stinks, love stinks
When is all about dough
Your love stinks to no money no honey.
Money and women don't get on well
Never have enough what do you expect
Demands it's all you get
Simple things they'll pay in bed
Buy me this, buy me that…
They never give a damn
Money and women don't get on well
When they are wearing pearls around their neck…
Money and women don't get on well
Thinks she is princess I can tell
Lipstick,make up and hairdressers
Fashion purses and mini skirts
Oh , Lords are you ready to hunt?
One man with lonely heart…
Money and women don't get on well
Spending money like a bat out of hell!!!
Love stinks, love stinks
When is all about dough
Your love stinks to no money no honey!!

⌗ Magick drops ⌗

Magick drops
Squat rules
Bruxelles truth
Ouija board
On full moon
Witch spells
Menstrual blood
Magick drops
Wiccan love
Ask the gnomes
For the rainbow
Where you can find the golden pot
Kept by Devon's leprechauns
Gigs of rock and roll
Menstrual blood
Magick drops
Wiccan love
Ask the gnomes
Where you can find
The Magick shrooms
On the fields
When the rain falls
You can see the leprechauns
Menstrual blood
Magick drops
Wiccan love
Welkome to my spot
Let me kill the roach

⫢ Irish Blood ⫢

When the smell to pain
Tears your guts apart
No worries is just
Honey sucked by the bee
From flowers it flies
To give another one's life
Irish Blood
Come home soon
Irish Blood
Flower in bloom
Now you can
Stretch your legs
And climb steps
Nothing to regret
In your life or your death
All I need is your faith
Irish Blood
Come home soon
Irish Blood
Flower in bloom
Best of your heart
Is your big pride
Kept in Pandora's box
Harder to get through
Than a bottomless pit hole
Carried as your Irish cross

Bohemian Paradise

Take me down to the paradise city
Where the grass is green and the girls are pretty
I want you please
Take me home
Domu sladke Domu
Home sweet home
Bohemian Paradise
Long away I left behind
Many friends and good looking girls
Times have changed but nothing else
I'm the same than when I left
Don't leave soon so far away
I've been waiting for my train
Stole my heart you little blue smurfs
Mushrooms picking in the dark
Magick plums make me drunk
I left crawling Singer pub
More than once, I swear to Lords
Magick plums make me drunk
Take me down to the paradise city
Where the grass is green and the girls are pretty
Domu sladke Domu
Home Sweet home
Bohemian Paradise
Found my way black is back
Nothing is free life is hard
Don't nag at me I had enough

Push my limits fucking bums
Please get lost don't suck my blood
Smoke alone in the sun
Dance with me I need a break
Jamming hard has been my game
Magick drums make me dance
I will tell you only once
Come with me will have some fun
Magick plums make me drunk
Take me down to the paradise city
Where the grass is green and the girls are pretty
Dance with me and have no shame
Like a wolf I howl my name
Magick plums make me drunk
Nothing that I should regret
Call me back please don't forget
Slivovitce makes me drunk
Drink with me you never learn
Something that you have to earn
Say nasdrovia and break the glass
Come with me we smoke some grass
Magick drums make me dance
Take me down to the paradise city
Where the grass is green and the girls are pretty

♯ Bye bye bye my sweet girl ♯

You gave me your heart

You gave me the strength

I wrote this song for your farewell

I wish your life would never end

But came your time my dear sweet friend

Bye bye bye my sweet girl

You came to me lonely and wet

And you became my best friend

I don't have words to say what I felt

You fought brave untill your fucking last breath

Bye bye bye my sweet girl

There will always be roses

In your dead bed

Bye bye golfa

⌗ Without Law ⌗

Giving away job
Body art is your work
Fighting against law
Riding your fire horse
Living without law
Riding your fire horse
Without law
Friends we became
After days of rain
When nobody cares
Laughs and tears we share
Living without law
Riding your fire horse
Without law
Hope to have you close
Needles and pain in my soul
Drawing my skins without law
Forever will be blood
Living without law
Riding your fire horse
Gypsy pride without law

⚡ Up and Downs ⚡

Psycho for you

I spoke the Truth

Met you was good

But break up is soon

Pictures I took

Nothing to lose

Life are ups and downs

We got it all

Thunders and storms

Blizzards of fun

The end is not far

Tears to the trash

For damned days we had

Life are ups and downs

Frames I took

When I was loved

Alone once more

The sun will go

On same spot

When I will be gone

⋕ Musuk ⋕

Black Cat in the hood

Chasing mice in the moon

Walking alone

Always bear foot

Black feet in my soul

Broke my heart real young

Always waiting for you to come soon

Black Cat in the moon

Saying meaow to the moon

Roaming around

All day long

Fooling nigga in the hood

Wild black Cat rules

Singing songs to the moon

Never knows when to come home

Chasing mice in the full moon

Black Cat in the hood

⌗ No Rush ⌗

Start your day early before rising sun

With a smile on your face

When your babes wake up

That kiss them and hug

Giving lots of fun

Courage don't need

Of that you have enough ¡!!

Go ahead, single mom

No rush to find your man

Finished your chores

Before the sun goes

Just after you had struggle with love

You are priceless,life made you gold

Please babes don't steal my heart

Go ahead, single mom

No rush to find your man

The night comes and you are sitting alone…

Smoking and thinking of what

You've done before

Nothing to worry you didn't

Make it wrong

That was your choice

To live on your own

No rush, no rush ¡!!

Go ahead single mom

No rush to find your man

Now you are living it large

Go ahead single mom

⚑ Lost Songs Darling ⚑

Psycodelik trip on my head

Trying to reach flying birds

If you don't come, I won't call you back

I go from here before smash your fucking bar

You are trash, trash ¡!!

Lost love songs on the way

Going back over my acid days

Why don't you let me be

Letting my soul to feel free

Psycodelik trip on my way

Why don't you jump in this night train to hell

It's leaving quarter to midnight

With the noise of the squeeze rails

Squeezing rails

Lost love songs in the rain

Always looking for new place to stay

Trying to crash out everyday

Feeling homeless in a train

Psycodelik trip on the rails

I saw you once fading away

Through a tunnel of white smoke

You were turning into a magick frog

Crock crock sing the frog

Lost love songs on a night train

Xmas dinner Louiza square

Running far was not fair

Come to me if you dare…

Psycodelik trip picking up again
I can't see where is the end
Come give me a hug
Making noises as a roaming cat
Meaow sings the cat
Lost love songs on the rails
Going downtown by a train
Better late than never to forget
All the bad trips and the hate
Psycodelik trip in my brain
I'm just feeling pain
After you broke my heart in a fun fair
Start to rock on a train
Rock rock does the train
Lost love songs on a grave
We can't scape from our fate
Nowhere to run when it's too late
I think there's life after death I should say
Psycodelik trip on a cold night
I feel as a cuckoo's bird
Trying to find where's the nest
On a night with thunders rain
I will make the rain
Lost love songs from my soul
Open your mind with acid drops
And look the life breaking through the door
Howling at the moon as a wolf ..!!
Waif wauf howlllll guau guau!!!!

⌗ No church no judge ⌗

Church Stinks
Inquisition sucks
Pagans praise
Goddess moon
Judge stinks
Court sucks
Justice is
unfair to me
No church no judge
Church Stinks
Inquisition sucks
Witch spells
Love mother Earth
Judge stinks
Court sucks
Free spirits
No jail will lock up
No church no judge
Church Stinks
Inquisition sucks
Christians prayers
Make no sense to me
Judge stinks
Court sucks
Blame me guilty
If you wish
No church no judge
Fuck church
Fuck judge
Lost souls you are
No church no judge

♯ Snow White Tales ♯

Long ago

Starts this Fairy tale

Seven Snow White

Fake friends

Poison apple

Given by a witch

And she felt asleep

Just wake up my queen

For years

Of darkness in a dream

Waiting for a kiss

From her blue Prince

Seven Snow White

Fake friends

Living in a dream

Just wake up my queen

Evil friends kept her in a dream

Waiting for a kiss

From her blue Prince

Seven Snow White

Fake friends

Living in a dream

Just wake up my queen

Evil friends

Kept her in a dream

Asking questions

To know who is the beautiest one

On the mirror

Lines of white dust

Years of work singing the darfs songs

Aijo, aijo,….aijo, aijo

Just wake up my queen

Blue Prince came

And kiss her lips

Wake up my queen

It's time to smile

We all know the end

Of this Fairy tale

Singing the darfs songs

Aijo, aijo, aijo, aijo….

Just wake up my queen

Seven Snow White

Fake friends

♯ Red Light District Stars ♯

Breathing love behind the glass
Babe your twenties won't last
Wish the time you could speed up...
Dancing around broken hearts
Where smells like money burnt
You were make of for lust
Got used to thinking fast
By Red Light District sluts
Jungle of love
Trading your flesh
For a couple blue notes
Red Light District Stars
Breathing love behind the glass
Lost my heart at red light bars
Whistling songs in the pubs
Night ladies are the stars
Waiting for me to return
With my heart broken apart
Full house and I don't bluff!!!
Ace and Queens in my hand
Jungle of love
Trading your flesh
For a couple blue notes
Red Light District Stars

Three Blue Notes of Lust

There blue notes of lust
To heal my broken heart
Like a shattered glass
You won't be the last
Babe you are my soul
When I look at you
I can see how far away
You have come through
There blue notes of lust
To heal my broken heart
Like a shattered glass
You won't be the last
Babe you and me
Can see the way we feel
With a pasional fruit
Lost in the garden of Eden
Three Blue Notes of Lust
To heal my broken heart
Like a shattered glass
You won't be the last

⌗ Gold Always Inside ⌗

Stash that shit up your ass
Gold Always Inside
It's not a safety ride
Keep your pride always inside
Gold Always Inside
Keep that on mind
It's a bumpy ride
Don't cross the line
You've been driving miles
Tank full of gas
For noisy ride
Let's start the fire
Gold Always Inside
Is a bumpy ride
In memory of Matt Griffith

⚥ Sunday Rules ⚥

Home alone
Sunday Rules
Set me free
Let me be
Home alone
The only thing
I want is
To be with you
Home alone
Sunday Rules
Making chores
All day long
Home alone
Come home soon
It's time to play
Good Rock and Roll
Home alone
Sunday Rules
Feeling lonely
Long ago
Since you were gone
In memory of my dad

✳ Flowers over a grave ✳

Lilly in my farm
Flowers over a grave
I won't forget my past
Don't regret anything of that
What I've done, I've done
Will never forget you
Your older grandson
Grandma you are
In my mind and blood
From wherever you are
Lilly in my farm
Flowers over a grave
Mary Jane look after my broken heart
I'm a shooting star

♯ Tonite is the night ♯

Tonite is the night
To Rock and Roll
Tonite is the night
To squat the world
Tonite is the night
To break the wall
Tonite is the night
We'll smoke it all
Tonite is the night
We break the laws
Tonite is the night
Of knights and Lords
Tonite is the night
We'll drink it all
Tonite is the nite
We fall in love
Tonite is the night
We Rock and Roll

⚡ Rathole ⚡

My hometown
Rathole town
By the beach
Most people stinks
From the castle
As a town hall
Churches preachers
My hometown
Rathole town
By the beach
Most people stinks
From their justice
And their beliefs
Crosses holders
Fuck your God
And your brotherhoods
Rats everywhere
Minding my business
Lick my balls
The way I like
Fucking fuggets
Fuck off and die
Rathole town
My hometown
By the beach
Most people stinks
My hometown
Rathole town

Shit Just Happened

Shit just happened since you were gone

I left you broken hearted and ditch you in a hole…

Tears I dropped empty my soul

Shit just happened since you were gone

Friends,lovers and familiars disappear

Slowly crossing the funnel tunnel

To the other side of the door

Fading off an energy of light….

Praise your Lords for new beginnings

On the eternal fight of good and evil

Against brain damage

Chemicals dwells

Life is a bipolar disorder itself

I don't care what your prophets said

They are just Maniac street preachers

To fight for the promise land

Inocentes and soldiers

Dying everywhere

Nothing worth much

To sacrifice your blood

For fuck sake leave me alone

Chasing my light to tell you

Who are you

Shit just happened since you were gone

You left me broken hearted

And ditch me in a hole

Shit just happened since you were gone